2

Power, Glory and
    Kingdom .
By John C Burt.

    Power
    Glory
    Kingdom
    Belong rightfully to
    The One who is to
    Come again.
    All power is vested
    In Him.
    All the Glory goes
    To Him.
    His Kingdom will
    Have no end.

    Power, Glory

And Kingdom
Started as a
Mustard seed
And has now grown
Into a big old
Tree covering many
Nations, tribes and
People's...

Power, Glory and
Kingdom will go on
And on stretching
Into an eternity.
Eternal life in the
Kingdom of God.
All Power, Glory
And the Kingdom
Rightfully belong
To Him who is

Coming again.

The Messiah,
The Son of God,
Jesus Christ.
All Power, Glory,
And the Kingdom
Belong rightfully unto
Him.
He did not consider
That he had all the
Power, Glory and
Authority...
He came to serve and
Be a servant ..

Died upon a cross
Of criminals.

Though He was
Innocent of any
Crime ....
The Lamb of God
Who takes away
The Sin of the World.
Power, Glory, and
Authority and the
Kingdom are
Rightfully His .....

Glory, Glory and Glory
In the Highest.
  By John C Burt.

  We say Glory, Glory,
  Glory, Gloria in
  Exclesis to the One
  Who is coming
  Again .
  Long may He reign
  and rule.
  Gloria Exclesis to the
  One who is the
   Great ' I AM '.

  The ' I AM ' who is
   God incarnate,

God in human form.
Come to Bethlehem
As a baby and after
33 years suffered, died
And rose again from the
Cross of Calvary.

Gloria Exclesis
Gloria Exclesis
Gloria Exclesis
Gloria Exclesis
To the One who
Is coming again.
To the One who
 Is coming again.
 To the One who
 Is coming again.

Glory in the Highest
To the One who is
Coming again.
Let the Highest Praises
Ring out across the
Earth ...
He is Worthy and due
All the Glory and Praise
We can bring Him .
He is The Way, The Truth
And The Life.
Gloria Exclesis.
Gloria Exclesis.
Gloria Exclesis.
Gloria Exclesis.

Give Him all the
Renown, honor

And Praise He
Is Worthy of !
Renown and all
Honor belong unto
Him alone.

There is no other One
Due His Glory, Renown
And Honor.
He all is worthy of all
Glory, Renown and
Honor.

Gloria Exclesis.
Gloria Exclesis.
Gloria Exclesis.
Gloria Exclesis.

Power, All Power
Belongs to Him.
  By John C Burt.

Power, All Power
Belongs to Him
Rightfully.
The One who is
Coming again
Has All Power
Vested in Himself.
The Father has given
Him All Power !
Power, All Power
Are rightfully His.

Power not as the
World knows it

Power to do the
Holy, Righteous and
Merciful actions He
Desires.

Power, absolute
Power corrupts
Except in the hands
Of the incorruptible
One who is coming
Again.
Power can make you
Drunk for more power.
Yet the Spotless One
 Is never drunk on
 His own power.
 Power, all power
 Belongs to Him,

Rightfully, rightfully.

Power, displayed as
In a storm coming over
The plains of Western
NSW.
Dark , threatening and
Full of power, lots of
Rain and wind in it..
An awesome display
Of the power of the One
Who is coming again..
An awesome display
Of the power of the One
Who is coming again ...
An awesome display
Of the power of the One
Who is coming again .....

After all He told
The Storm on Lake
Galilee to be quiet
And to be stilled.
Such a display of
Power and Control
Over the forces of
Creation.

Power, All Power
Belongs to Him
Rightfully, the One
Who is coming
Again ......

Kingdom, Thy
Kingdom Come.
  By John C Burt.

Kingdom come
Your Kingdom
Come !
So we all pray
Your Kingdom come
Upon the Earth and
All the Creation and
Soon, soon.
Kingdom, thy Kingdom
Come, Kingdom,
Thy Kingdom Come.

Kingdom your rule
and reign over the

World and all
Creation.
Reign and rule
Of the Lord most
High.
Reign and rule
Of the Lord most
High.
Reign and rule
Of the Lord most
High.

Kingdom, thy Kingdom
Come.
Kingdom rule begins
In the here and now.
The power, glory
and authority and

Kingdom belong
Rightfully to you alone.

Kingdom, reign and
Rule of the One
Who is coming again.
Long may He reign and
Rule over us, the World
And the entire Creation.
His Kingdom will know
No end.
His reign and rule
Go on for an eternity.
An eternity under the
Reign and rule and power
And authority of the Lord
Almighty .....

Reign and rule, and
Power, glory and
Authority and the
Kingdom that will
Have no end.
May the Kingdom come
Quickly, its been growing
And growing, unnoticed
by
Many.

Thy Kingdom come.
Thy Kingdom come.
Thy Kingdom come.
Thy Kingdom come.

Kingdom, Thy Kingdom
Come. Come quickly ...

Authority, Power, Glory
And Kingdom.
By John C Burt.

The Man from Galilee
Said ' All authority has
Been given unto me by
My Father in heaven.'
All authority, means
All authority.
There is nothing
Outside of the Man
From Galilee.
He is the One who
Has all authority on
Heaven and Earth.

We have authority

When we walk in
His name.
We have authority
When we walk in
His name.
We have authority
When we walk in
His name.

All authority vested
By the Father in the
Man from Galilee.
All authority, His
Authority has no
Rivals or rival
Authority.
All authority vested
By the Father in the
Man from Galilee.

His reign, rule, power,
And authority will know
No end, they go on, and on,
And on, for an eternity
With God the Father, the
Son and the Holy Spirit.

All authority, eternal
Authority, to reign
And rule over the
Earth, Universe and
All Creation.
His Kingdom come, His
Rule and reign will have
No end !

Authority, Power, Glory
And Kingdom will come

And rightfully belong to
The One who is to come
Again.
Rightfully belong to
The One who is to
Come again.
Rightfully belong to
The One who is to
Come again.

Rightful King, with
Kingdom, Power, and
Authority and All
Glory ......

Verse By Verse.
By John C Burt.

Verse by verse
Kingdom and Power
And Glory are seen
Verse by verse.
Word upon word.
Its plain to see if
You look.
Kingdom, Power
And authority
Belong unto Him.

Word upon word
Verse upon verse
So the His - Story

Of the Father, the
Son and the Holy
Spirit goes on and
Grows , going on
Forever, and forever,
And forever.

Verse upon verse
Truth upon truth
Words upon words
Light upon light.
Darkness has to flee
In the face of
Verse upon verse
Scripture upon
Scripture.

All scripture verses

Are profitable to
The Man and Woman
Of God, training up,
And teaching them.
Verse upon verse.
Truth upon truth.

He will lead us into
All truth.
Verse upon verse.
Verse upon verse.
Verse upon verse.
Truth upon truth.
Truth upon truth.
Truth upon truth.
Verse by verse.

Verse upon verse
Percept upon percept.
Building a Spiritual
House, His Kingdom,
Power, Glory, and
Authority will have
No end.

Verse upon verse.
Verse upon verse.
Verse upon verse.
Stacked up high.
Verse by verse.
Verse by verse.
Verse by verse.